Good Question!

Did Christopher Columbus
Really Discover America?

AND OTHER QUESTIONS ABOUT
The New World

STERLING CHILDREN'S BOOKS
New York

STERLING CHILDREN'S BOOKS
New York

An Imprint of Sterling Publishing
387 Park Avenue South
New York, NY 10016

Text © 2014 by Emma Carlson Berne
Illustrations © 2014 by Sterling Publishing Co, Inc.

10 left: Library of Congress; 10 right: © Duncan P Walker/iStockphoto; 17 left: © Victor Boswell/National Geographic; 17 center: Center for the Study of the History of Mexico Carso/ Courtesy Wikimedia Foundation; 17 right: © picstodisc/iStockphoto; 18: Courtesy Wikimedia Foundation; 27: © North Wind Picture Archives/Alamy; 28: Museo Nacional de Arte/Courtesy Wikimedia Foundation

ISBN 978-1-4549-1258-3 [hardcover]
ISBN 978-1-4549-1259-0 [paperback]

Distributed in Canada by Sterling Publishing
c/o Canadian Manda Group, 165 Dufferin Street
Toronto, Ontario, Canada M6K 3H6
Distributed in the United Kingdom by GMC Distribution Services
Castle Place, 166 High Street, Lewes, East Sussex, England BN7 1XU
Distributed in Australia by Capricorn Link (Australia) Pty. Ltd.
P.O. Box 704, Windsor, NSW 2756, Australia

Design by Andrea Miller
Paintings by Robert Barrett

For information about custom editions, special sales, and premium and corporate purchases, please contact
Sterling Special Sales at 800-805-5489 or specialsales@sterlingpublishing.com.

Manufactured in China
Lot #:
2 4 6 8 10 9 7 5 3 1
10/14

www.sterlingpublishing.com/kids

CONTENTS

What was the New World?

In the year 986, a Viking explorer named Bjarni Herjolfsson was blown off course between Iceland and Greenland. Eventually, he spotted the shores of a distant, unknown land. When Herjolfsson finally found his way back to Greenland, an interested Viking explorer named Leif Eriksson heard his story. He set out with a crew to find this new land.

Eriksson succeeded. He made his way to what is now the northern coast of Canada. Eriksson and his men wanted to set up a colony in this new land. They sailed home, bringing back men, women, and animals.

But people already lived in this new land: Native Americans whom the Vikings called *skraelings*. The two groups clashed almost immediately. The Vikings killed eight Native Americans. The Native Americans retaliated, attacking settlers. Eventually, the Vikings abandoned their settlements. Their huts crumbled into dust, and over the next 500 years many people forgot the Viking settlements ever existed.

To the Vikings, this new land was a strange and distant place. But for thousands of years the New World was filled with dancing, ball games, wars, music, fishing, farming, council meetings, travel, marriages, births, and deaths. In other words, the "New World"—what Europeans called North America and South America—was just like all other places that humans have ever lived.

Across the Atlantic Ocean was the "Old World"—Europe. By the late fifteenth century, Europeans had traveled to Africa and even to China and parts of Asia, which they called the Indies. In 1271, an Italian explorer named Marco Polo went east to China and brought back stories of amazing riches. But the only known way to this part of the world was either by sailing along the coast of Southeast Asia and India or overland—both long and difficult journeys. European explorers wanted to find an easier way. Perhaps they could travel west through the open sea, some thought.

At this time, the Old World and the New World were completely unknown to each other. But that would soon change.

Native Americans lived in the New World long before European explorers arrived there.

Who was Christopher Columbus?

Christopher Columbus was born in 1451 and lived in the busy town of Genoa, in present-day Italy. He had a father, Domenico, and a mother, Susanna, and four siblings: Bartolomeo, Giovanni, Giocomi, and Bianchinetta. His father wove and sold wool for a living. Like most merchants at the time, Domenico and his family lived and worked in the same house. Their wool workshop was probably in one room and their living area in another. From what we know, Columbus had a very normal childhood for the time. But his life probably seems very different from yours.

Many boys, especially those who were poorer, did not go to school. Girls did not go to school at all. At school, boys were expected to sit and study for many hours without recess. The master, as the teacher was called, would ask questions about what they had learned. Wrong answers would mean getting beaten with a stick or a bundle of sticks.

In many ways, children in Columbus's time were treated like little adults. They were expected to work at a job, usually assisting their parents. They might help to plow fields, plant and harvest crops, butcher animals, cook meals, and sew clothes. Columbus probably spent many hours sorting and cleaning wool in his father's workshop.

The town of Genoa was a thriving seaport. All his life, Columbus had watched ships sail in and out of the harbor. He didn't come from a poor background, but Columbus didn't want to be a weaver like his father. He wanted to be an explorer. He had read about Marco Polo's travels to the Indies, and he craved the riches and adventure that the Italian explorer had found. Columbus would indeed find adventure in his life: he is famous today for sailing back and forth between Europe and the Americas. He established a sea route that others could use, and he set up communities, or settlements, that were the start of today's cities.

How did Christopher Columbus learn to sail ships?

When he was fourteen, Christopher Columbus left home to become an apprentice on a trading ship. During medieval times, between the fifth and fifteenth centuries, becoming an apprentice was the way young men learned a profession. Apprentices were like trainees. They were paid a small amount and learned their employer's trade. Columbus most likely learned about handling big boats when he sailed his employer's ships on long trading voyages to the Greek isles. Older, more experienced sailors would have taught him how to estimate distances just by sight, how to anchor a ship, and how to steer through currents in narrow passageways. But apprentices also did some of the hardest and most dangerous work, such as climbing the tallest mast to roll or unroll a sail. An apprentice would also have to empty the pump that kept the ship from taking on too much water. This was a physically difficult task and so smelly that sailors sometimes fainted from the stench.

Why did explorers want to cross the ocean to get to the New World?

There were many stories about the wealthy and powerful Asian ruler, the Great Khan, and the riches he had amassed in China. Some said he had palaces with floors of gold three inches thick and rubies as big as a man's fist. Many of these stories had been brought back by Marco Polo. He had met the Great Khan and had seen his fabulous wealth.

The route Marco Polo traveled was called the Silk Road. Since almost 500 BCE, travelers had used this series of routes between what is now Europe, India, the Middle East, and China. But Marco Polo had traveled to the Indies almost two hundred years before Columbus's time. Since then, the Ottoman Empire controlled many of the Silk Road routes and made them extremely difficult for Europeans to use. Columbus and other explorers thought that if they could just find a way to *sail* to the Indies, as this region was often called, they could bring back gold, jewels, and spices.

The Known World in 1492

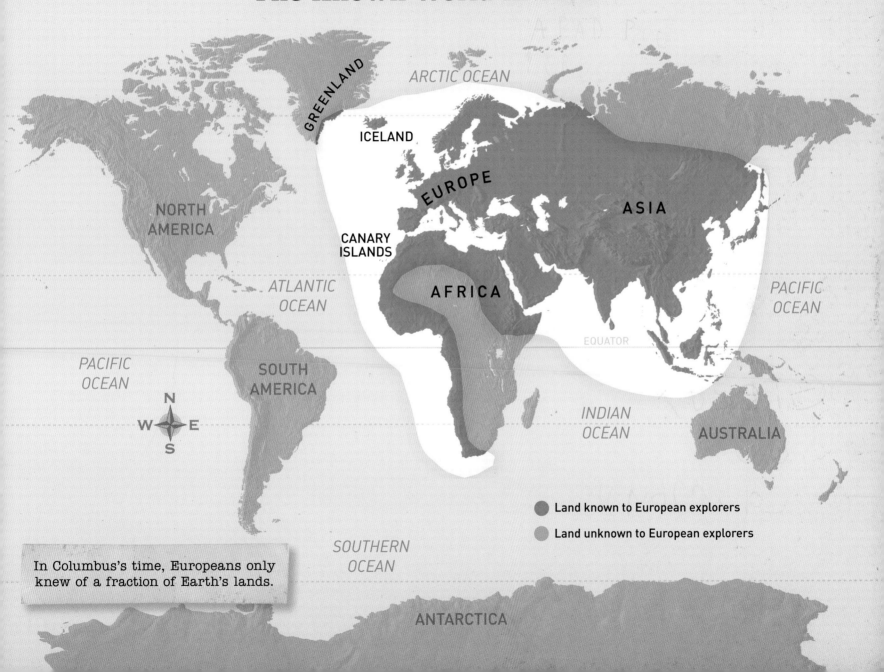

ARCTIC OCEAN

GREENLAND

ICELAND

EUROPE

ASIA

NORTH AMERICA

CANARY ISLANDS

AFRICA

ATLANTIC OCEAN

PACIFIC OCEAN

EQUATOR

PACIFIC OCEAN

SOUTH AMERICA

INDIAN OCEAN

AUSTRALIA

N
W E
S

SOUTHERN OCEAN

ANTARCTICA

Land known to European explorers

Land unknown to European explorers

In Columbus's time, Europeans only knew of a fraction of Earth's lands.

Queen Isabella and King Ferdinand gave
Columbus the ships and crew to sail the world.

Who helped Columbus on his quest?

Columbus wanted to do what no one had ever done before: sail west to end up in the Indies. But he couldn't just set sail in one day. Columbus needed ships, food, water, equipment, and a crew. To get all of this, he would need a patron, someone who would provide money.

Columbus spent eight years asking the kings and queens of various countries to fund his trip. Finally, Queen Isabella and King Ferdinand of what is now known as Spain decided to give Columbus a chance. They agreed to give him ships, a crew, and provisions, in exchange for most of the profits he brought back. Columbus would also claim any lands he found for Spain, making it more powerful. If he succeeded, Columbus would receive an official title: Admiral of the Ocean Sea.

The king and queen ordered the small port town of Palos to provide two ships and supplies. Later, Columbus arranged to rent a third ship. He found two excellent captains—the Pinzón brothers, Martín Alonso and Vicente Yañez. Between eighty-six and eighty-nine men and boys logged on as crew members. Most of them were regular sailors who would be responsible for the daily workings of the ships. Columbus also took along carpenters, barrel makers, caulkers (leak repairers), a secretary, a surgeon, and an interpreter to communicate with the Great Khan. At least two ships had cabin boys who cleaned, took care of the gear, and also turned the ship's hourglass, which kept track of time.

Columbus had a hard time finding sailors to go with him. Many people believed that he would fail and die at sea. But a few old-timers believed in Columbus. The Pinzóns were respected in the seafaring community. Once the brothers agreed to captain the ships, other sailors were more willing to sign on. In addition, Isabella and Ferdinand offered prisoners a chance to get out of their sentences if they went with Columbus. Four criminals took the offer. Finally, Columbus had his crew.

CARAVEL

How did Columbus cross the ocean?

By 1492, Columbus was ready to start his long journey. Columbus and his crew would cross the ocean in two smaller ships, called caravels, named the *Pinta* and the *Niña*, and one larger ship, or nao, called the *Santa María*. These three massive wooden ships each measured about seventy feet (about the length of two school buses), and they were technologically advanced for the time. The caravels were more nimble, narrower, and sat higher in the water than the nao. They were also faster, easier to steer, and could maneuver closer to coastlines. But the nao was a sturdier ship with much more room for cargo. The *Santa María* was the flagship, which is the main ship that carries the commander and bears a flag. But all through his journey Columbus complained that it was slow and clumsy. The smaller, swifter *Niña* was his favorite ship.

Like all ships at the time, Columbus's vessels had no motors or engines. They were powered entirely by a complex set of sails that could be raised, lowered, and turned to harness the wind that moved the ship forward. When the wind wasn't blowing, ships could be becalmed, meaning they were stuck floating with no way to move forward until the wind picked up. In fact, very soon after Columbus began his journey, his ships were becalmed for several days just a few miles off the coast.

On August 3, 1492, the ships left Palos harbor. Their first stop was the Canary Islands, about nine hundred miles off the coast of Spain. Columbus knew that strong ocean winds blew west off the coast of the Canaries. They could pick up these winds and be on their way. On September 6, 1492, they did just that. Heading west-southwest, the *Santa María*, the *Pinta*, and the *Niña* and all their crew sailed away from the Canaries, away from Europe—and toward a future no one could guess.

What was life like on the *Niña*, the *Pinta*, and the *Santa María*?

Daily life on a medieval ship was very different from life on a modern ship. Today, sailors have cabins and bunks to sleep in with sheets and blankets. There are heating and air-conditioning, bathrooms, showers, and fully equipped kitchens. People spend weeks aboard cruise ships for enjoyment. But sailing on a medieval ship was far from fun.

One of the biggest problems was keeping food fresh and protecting it from rodents and insects that infested the ships. Columbus brought along salted meat, cheese, chickpeas, lentils, raisins, oil, and beans. The sailors would season their food with huge amounts of fresh garlic to mask the rotten taste. Each sailor had to do his own cooking, too, because ships didn't have a cook in those days. Crew members cooked their food over fires made in sandboxes on the deck to make sure they didn't accidentally set the ship on fire. They probably preferred to wait until after dark to eat, so they wouldn't have to see the maggots and other insects that were crawling in their food.

The crew slept on the open deck, which must have been constantly wet with the ocean's spray. Only the captain of each ship had a tiny cabin, just big enough for a bed and a table. There was no plumbing of any kind. Everyone relieved himself by squatting on a wooden seat that extended over the side of the ship.

Life on the ships was cramped, dirty, and uncomfortable. By the journey's end, nearly every man was surely crawling with lice and fleas. But this was a normal life for a sailor in the fifteenth century—no one was surprised by these conditions, and no one expected anything better.

How did Columbus navigate the ocean?

Of course, in 1492 Columbus didn't use GPS navigation or a radio or radar. He didn't have any of the modern tools that sea captains use today. Instead, Columbus navigated by studying the position of the stars in the night sky. By keeping track of the North Star, he could judge approximately in which direction he was heading. He calculated how fast the ships were going by tossing a knotted rope into the water at the front of the ship. The sailors used an hourglass to measure how long the rope took to pass the ship in the water.

How long did it take to cross the ocean?

The entire journey took seventy days. From the beginning, the sailors were nervous about how far they would be traveling from land. Columbus kept two records with two different distances. Some scholars believe that Columbus was deliberately showing his men false numbers, so they would not be frightened by how far they were sailing. Others have said that Columbus was simply using two different measurements of distance, and showing the crew the measurement that they would be most familiar with.

Life on the ships followed a strict routine. Sailors rotated sailing and lookout duties. They prayed at set times, scrubbed and cleared off the deck and railings, and cleaned off slimy mildew. They also loosened, tightened, raised, and lowered the sails at the captain's command. When they were working, they sang songs. The rhythm helped everyone to work together.

The sailors had about four hours of free time after their shift was done. They would try to sleep, tell stories to one another, or fish over the side of the ship. Sometimes, they would sing and play flutes or drums while others danced.

Finally, on October 12, after seventy days at sea, the lookout on the *Pinta* called "*Tierra! Tierra!*" ("Land, land!") They had made it. But where were they?

Columbus used knotted rope to measure his ships' speed and a compass to guide him. You can also see a letter in Columbus's own handwriting.

Christopher Columbus *was* the first European captain to command an expedition, establish settlements that survived, and return to Europe. In fact, Columbus sailed back and forth from Europe to the Americas four times. More and more settlers followed him. Eventually, colonies were set up, which provided the basis for the North America we know today.

Columbus had discovered a part of the world that was previously unknown to Europeans. But thousands of people were already living in the Americas when he arrived. These were the ancestors of the people we know today as Native Americans. In the north, these were the native people the Vikings called *skraelings*. Columbus never journeyed to what is today the mainland United States or Canada. Instead, he and his sailors landed on the shores of what is now called the Bahamas. There, he met a group of people called the Taínos. The islands of the Bahamas were the Taínos' home. They had come from the area around what is now Venezuela as a part of a large migration of people beginning about 400 BCE. These people gradually traveled through the Caribbean islands, where they settled among and mixed with people who already lived there. Different communities developed on various islands that we know now as Haiti, the Dominican Republic, the Bahamas, Cuba, Jamaica, and the Virgin Islands.

Columbus thought he had achieved his goal—that he was indeed in the Indies. He was both right and wrong. He had done what he set out to do: sailed west and found land. But he wasn't in the Indies, and this land was only a discovery for the Europeans, not to the people who already lived there.

This oil painting by Michael Zeno Diemer shows Columbus sailing the *Santa María* in rough seas.

The Taíno people lived in a peaceful world of water and sand, misty forests, low mountains, rivers, and lakes. Lush with plants and teeming with small mammals, the islands were gentle, friendly places to live. The Taíno people had thrived there for close to two thousand years and were over three million in number.

They lived in grass huts scented with bundles of sweet-smelling plants, decorated with strips of bark twisted into patterns, and covered with roofs of leaves. Each person had a cotton-and-grass hammock to sleep in. The Taínos grew sweet potatoes, squash, beans, and manioc, which is similar to yams. The islands had no large mammals such as horses or cows. But the Taínos were excellent fisherman. They built canoes out of giant trees—some big enough to carry 150 men. In these boats, the Taínos hunted manatees and giant sea turtles using only spears. They also built huge underwater pens woven out of reeds that fenced off sections of shoreline. This kept thousands of fish nearby, so they had plenty to eat.

The mild island climate and the Taínos's successful farming and hunting gave them time to make art out of bone and wood, weave belts and hammocks from dyed cotton, play elaborate ball games, and hold dances. The Taínos did not have a written language, but they had a sophisticated government. Each village was governed by a chief, called a *cacique*. Both men and women could become *caciques*. The chiefs were overseen by a head *cacique*. Huts were grouped around a large open area, used for dances, meetings, and ball games. The *cacique*'s house stood in the middle.

The Taínos were advanced. They did not enslave others or force labor. They knew how to make rubber, cyanide, and a form of pepper gas for their occasional wars. They developed a large variety of medicines from plants. They also made elaborate pottery and decorated their bodies and objects with images of their gods and other spiritual figures.

Why did Columbus call the people he met "Indians"?

Columbus was sure that he had reached the Indies and that the people he saw were subjects of the Great Khan. Therefore, he thought, they must be "Indians." Of course, they were not. The Indies were still eight thousand miles away.

As soon as Columbus stepped off the boat that had carried him and his party from the ships, he made a declaration that he was taking possession of these lands on behalf of Ferdinand and Isabella. This was the accepted way of claiming land in Columbus's culture. The thought that these lands were not his to take would not have occurred to him. Small groups of Taínos gathered on the beach, staring in astonishment at these newcomers. Columbus noted in his journal, "They are very well made with very handsome bodies, and very good [faces]." Many of the men were naked, he wrote, and wore their hair cut into bangs in the front and long in the back. When he saw women, Columbus observed that many of them went naked as well. Later, Columbus observed women wearing short skirts, flaps of cloth, or leaves to cover themselves, and other adults wearing short cotton cloaks.

We don't know what the Taínos thought of the Europeans, but they must have been utterly astonished by these strange men. The Europeans wore heavy wool clothes that covered their whole bodies except for their hands, necks, and heads. The Taínos had never seen people who were so covered up, especially since it was so hot in the tropical climate. They had never seen swords, Columbus noted, because when they were shown the weapons, they grasped them by the blades and cut themselves. And the Taínos had certainly never seen such huge ships with massive sails.

The two cultures stood on that beach, staring at each other, both unaware that this meeting—this day—would change the world forever.

Columbus's men and the Taínos were friendly at first.

How did the native people treat Columbus and his men?

A story with two sides isn't complete if only one side gets to speak. But unfortunately we do not know what the Taínos thought, we only know what Columbus and other Europeans wrote.

At that first meeting, the Taínos treated the Europeans as guests. They led the Europeans to their villages, presented them to their *cacique*, and fed them. Later, the Taínos brought out items to trade and offered places to sleep in their own homes. The Taínos seemed amazed by these new people. Columbus noted how excited the Taínos were. The crew were always offered food and drink, as well as trade goods. Some Taínos threw themselves on the ground or raised their arms to the sky at the sight of the Europeans. Columbus interpreted these actions as giving thanks to God, but we cannot know what the Taínos meant.

How did Columbus treat the native people?

The first interactions between these two cultures were peaceful. But co-existence was not what Columbus had in mind.

He was not interested in the parrots, spears, and cotton the Taínos offered in trade. He wanted to profit from the islands and their people. Marco Polo had described the incredible wealth of the Great Khan. But as the crew spent more time on the islands, Columbus must have begun to realize that, wherever they were, they were *not* in the Indies. Nevertheless, Columbus noted that some of the people wore small gold jewelry. That meant there was gold on the islands, which he could take. He also noted that the Taíno people had very few weapons compared to Europeans. Columbus reported back to the king and queen that Taínos were not skilled with arms. The Taínos could be fierce warriors, but they were no match for the swords and knives of the Europeans. Columbus wrote to Ferdinand and Isabella, telling them how easy it would be to enslave the Taínos: "with fifty men they can all be subjugated [controlled] and made to do what is required of them."

What happened to the Taíno people after Columbus arrived?

Within two months of Columbus's arrival, he had set up the first fort, La Navidad. Columbus traveled back and forth to the New World four times. Other ships bringing many settlers followed his route.

This was the beginning of the end of the Taíno people and their culture. By the early 1500s, 85 percent of the Taíno population had died, either in fighting, by suicide, murder, or disease. Those who were left fled to other areas beyond European control. By the 1530s, very few full-blooded Taínos remained.

Columbus and those who followed him were obsessed by the promise of gold. By early 1495, 1,600 Taínos had been captured as slaves. Five hundred were loaded onto ships to be sold in Spain. Enslaving Taínos became a regular way of life. The captives were forced to farm and provide for the European settlers. Others were made to search for gold.

Those who did not find enough gold faced severe punishment—some were beaten. Some even had a hand cut off or were killed. Others died in the fields where they were forced to work. The Taínos fought back many times over the years, but those who rebelled were killed. Life had become brutal and miserable. But by far the biggest killer of the Taíno people was accidental: smallpox.

Why did so many native people die of disease?

The disease smallpox had existed for generations among Europeans. Sometimes victims died, and sometimes they lived. The Europeans had some immunity, or resistance, to smallpox and other diseases like measles, dysentery, typhus, and tuberculosis. But without knowing it, sailors carried these germs to the New World. When they interacted with the Taínos, the germs spread. The Taíno population had no resistance of any kind to these diseases, and people began to die very quickly. No medicines were available to help them—or anyone afflicted during this time in history.

In this woodcut, native people wash gold as they toil under Spanish rule.

What happened to Columbus when he returned to Spain?

Columbus was greeted as a hero when he returned to Spain. He had done what he said he would—sailed west, found land, and claimed it for Spain. Although he had not met the Great Khan or brought back boatloads of gold, spices, and jewels, he was sure he would find these riches in time. Queen Isabella and King Ferdinand shared his confidence. They awarded him the title he had been promised: Admiral of the Ocean Sea. They made him governor of the colonies. Columbus was paraded through the streets and treated as a celebrity. Seventeen ships were sent back with him on his second journey to the New World.

But as the years passed and it became clear that Columbus had neither reached the Indies nor discovered a land overflowing with riches, the nobles became unhappy with their hero. Columbus's settlements in the Americas were disorganized, and his own men rebelled against his leadership. The settlers stole from, fought, and even killed one another. They were hungry for gold, and Columbus could not control them.

As for Columbus himself, he became sick and needy. He always saw himself as a great discoverer. He was forever asking the monarchs for more money and ships so he could go on more expeditions. He was, after all, the Admiral of the Ocean Sea. Eventually, Columbus was removed as leader of the settlements. He spent his last years following the Spanish court as they traveled from one place to another. He believed he had been denied money, titles, and honor by the Spanish monarchs, and he had gathered together all the letters and documents that proved this. Columbus called these papers the *Book of Privileges*. As he neared death, Columbus wrote endless letters to one of his sons. He demanded his son to ask the monarchs for the money he believed they owed him. But the money and honor were not restored. Columbus died on May 20, 1506. Few noticed.

This painting by Juan Cordero shows Columbus presenting kidnapped Taínos to Ferdinand and Isabella.

How did Columbus change the world?

The planet would never be the same after Columbus. Two parts of the world that had been separated were now joined forever—for better or for worse.

Plants and animals traveled back and forth between the Old World and the New World. Horses were brought on ships to the New World by the Europeans who followed Columbus. European settlement expanded into what would become the United States. Native American tribes living there adopted the horse. The animal's speed and ability to travel long distances shaped Native culture for the next 500 years. In turn, the sailors saw Native people smoking odd little bundles of dried leaves. Tobacco made the journey back to Europe, and smoking was introduced to the wider world.

From Spain, settlers brought sugarcane, wheat, olives, oranges, lemons, cucumbers, lettuce, and melons. They brought animals that had never existed in the New World, including horses, cattle, sheep, goats, some types of dogs, and pigs.

Corn, white potatoes, sweet potatoes, pineapple, tomatoes, avocado, chili peppers, cacao beans, squash, and peanuts were all brought back by sailors and introduced to Europeans, who viewed these new foods with wonder and suspicion. This trade of plants and animals has been so important to the world that it even has its own name: the Columbian Exchange.

For most of the last 500 years, modern American people have been taught to see Columbus as a dashing explorer and the man who "discovered America." An American federal holiday is named for him, as well as many streets, cities, squares, and buildings. Behind Columbus's name lie two continents and a nation but also a wave of violence. His legacy is complicated. He was a brilliant sailor but also a ruthless and sometimes dishonest leader. Columbus and the settlers helped shape the modern world but, horrifically, they wiped out the Taíno people. A villain to some, a hero to others, Columbus was a flawed and mortal man. His legacy will never be forgotten.

NEW WORLD TIMELINE

400 BCE — Taíno ancestors migrate from area around present-day Venezuela. Eventually, they settle on the islands of the Caribbean.

1000 CE (approximate) — The Viking explorer Leif Eriksson sails to a land he calls Vinland, somewhere on the North American coast near Newfoundland. The settlement he founded does not survive.

1271 — Marco Polo travels overland through Europe and Asia to the Indies, where he meets the Great Khan and sees the wealth of his empire.

1451 — Christopher Columbus is born in Genoa, Italy.

1492 — Columbus sails from Europe and reaches the New World. He believes he is in the Indies, on the coast of Asia. He meets the Taíno people, whom he calls "Indians."

1493 — Columbus makes a second voyage to the New World. He returns to Portugal in 1496.

1498 — Columbus leaves Spain for a third voyage to the New World.

1500 — Columbus is removed as governor of the colonies under accusations of mismanagement.

1502 — Columbus departs Spain for a fourth and final voyage to the New World. He becomes stranded in present-day Jamaica. He is rescued and sent home to Europe, arriving in 1502.

1506 — After four voyages to the New World and much controversy and bloodshed, Columbus dies in Spain.

1520 (approximate) — The first recorded outbreak of smallpox among the Taíno people begins the decline of the population.

1530s (approximate) — Eighty-five percent of the Taíno population has died or fled, signaling the end of the Taíno society.

For bibliography and further reading visit www.sterlingpublishing.com/good-question